Camping Kit

Written by
Cath Jones

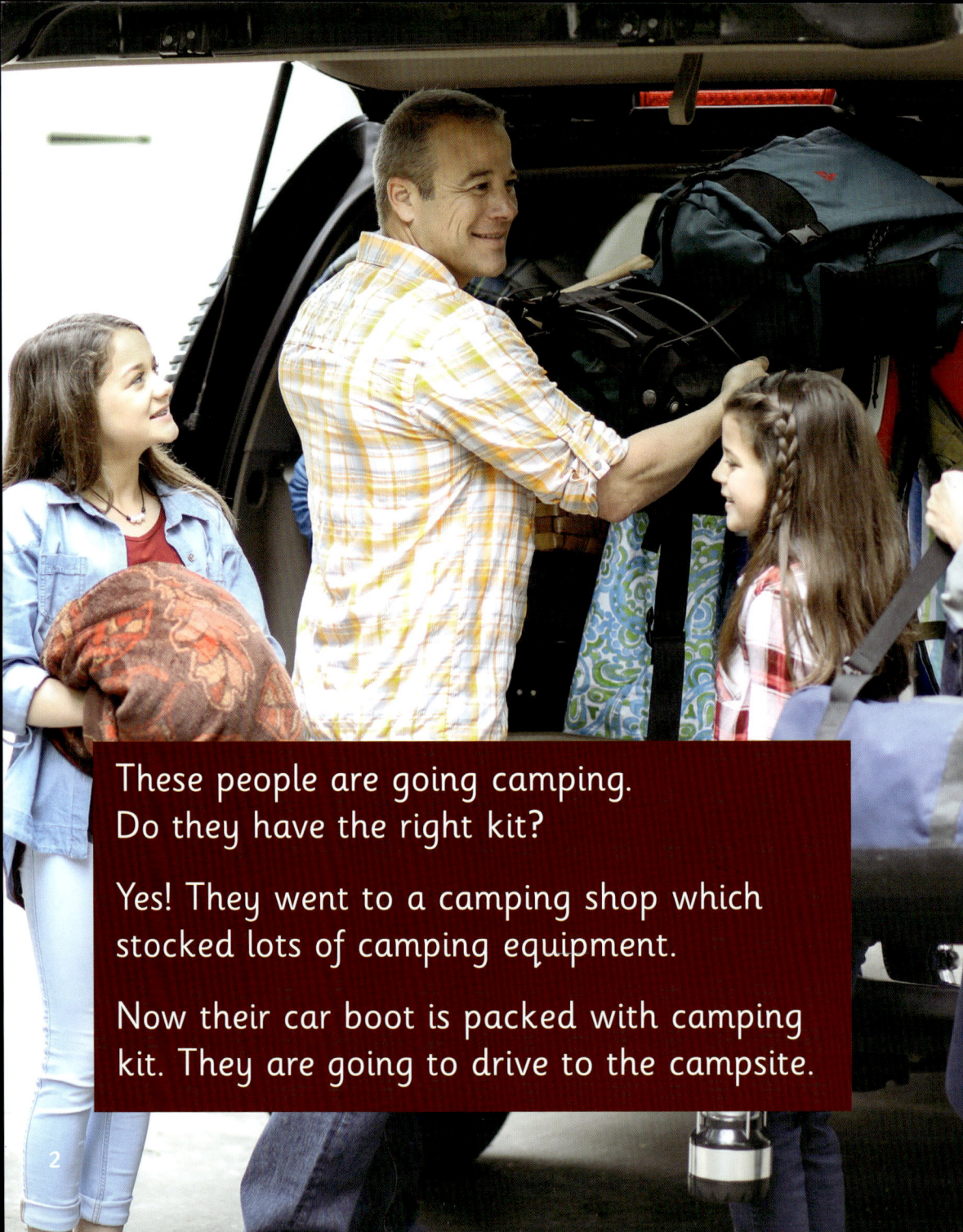

These people are going camping. Do they have the right kit?

Yes! They went to a camping shop which stocked lots of camping equipment.

Now their car boot is packed with camping kit. They are going to drive to the campsite.

These people have fitted all their camping kit into a boat.

Dave has all his kit in a rucksack on his back.

You can camp outside on a campsite or at home in the garden. You can even camp inside.

Some people camp in camper vans. Some people like tents.

Tents can be erected in odd spots.

Look at this man. His tent is hanging from a rock. That is extreme camping!

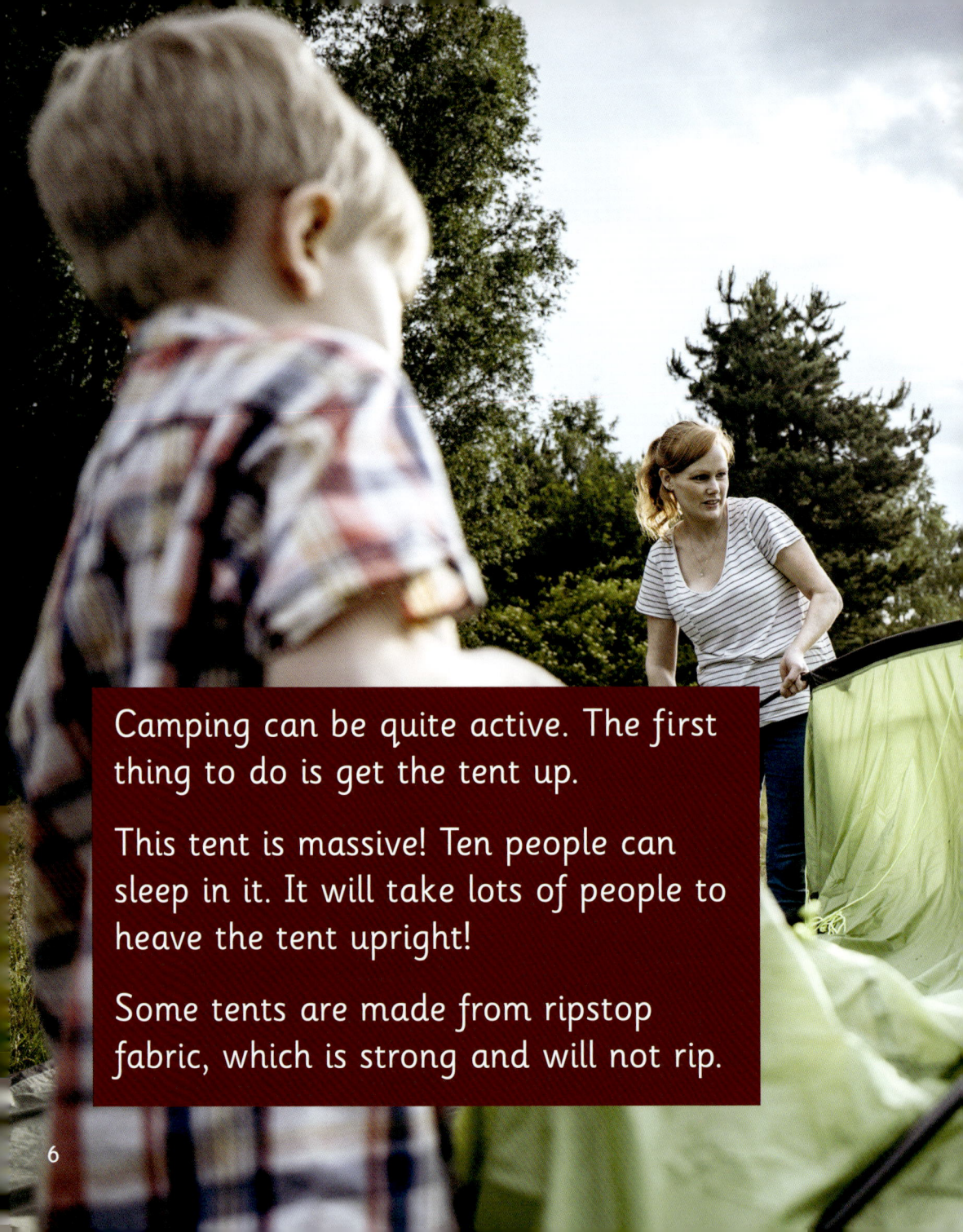

Camping can be quite active. The first thing to do is get the tent up.

This tent is massive! Ten people can sleep in it. It will take lots of people to heave the tent upright!

Some tents are made from ripstop fabric, which is strong and will not rip.

There are five poles to keep the tent up.

The tent pegs are made of steel.

Sometimes pegs are made of plastic. But when you hammer tent pegs into the ground, plastic ones can snap if the ground is too hard.

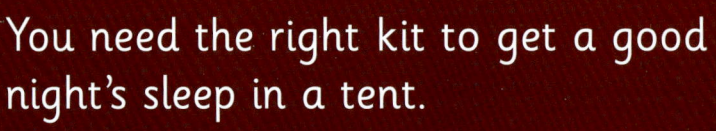

You need the right kit to get a good night's sleep in a tent.

A thick sleeping bag will keep you snug. This goes on top of a sleep mat or an air mattress.

A torch or a lamp will help you see at night.

Cooking when you are camping can be a lot of fun.

You can cook on a camping stove or on a campfire.

Gas stoves have a valve. An adult can turn the valve and light the gas.

A camping stove is splendid for cooking outside in the fresh air. But you must **never** cook inside a tent.

If you have the right kit, camping can be a good time to have a rest.

A hammock is just right for hanging out in.

These dads have camping chairs.

Some people take their pets camping.

This cat has the right kit for camping in the wet. It has a camping coat to keep it snug!

This dog is just staying out of the rain.

Some people like posh camping. They even sleep in a proper bed!

This is called **glamping**.

These people do not need to bring much camping kit.